Accent on Analytical
Sonatinas

by William Gillock

To Esther Mills Wood

FOREWORD

Your ability to project the meaning of the music you play depends upon the degree to which you understand *how* the composer has constructed the piece.

The work of the composer may be classified in two broad categories – **art** and **craft**. How much of the former you understand depends on your own sensitivity to the language of music. Art, in any form, cannot be described in mere words, for our spoken languages are far too limited. However, the craft of the composer can be analyzed.

To understand one phase of this craft, i.e., "form," you must know that the composer works with only three basic materials:

1. REPETITION   2. CONTRAST   3. VARIATION

Musical forms have been developed by the planned placement of REPEATED ideas in relation to CONTRASTING and VARYING ideas.

At the beginning of each movement of the following sonatinas you will find an outline of the form. As you study each movement, identify the various divisions of the form in the music.

William Gillock

CONTENTS

2   First Sonatina
- I. Moderato grazioso
- II. Andante
- III. Rondo: Vivace

8   Second Sonatina
- I. Allegro
- II. Moderato cantabile
- III. Rondo: Allegro vivace

16   Third Sonatina
- I. Allegretto grazioso
- II. Tempo di menuetto
- III. Rondo: Spiritoso vivace

ISBN 978-1-4584-2194-4

EXCLUSIVELY DISTRIBUTED BY

WILLIS MUSIC

HAL•LEONARD®

Visit Hal Leonard Online at
www.halleonard.com

First Sonatina

I

SONATA FORM

Exposition
    M. T. — Main theme

Development
    D. G. — Development Group
        based on M. T.

Recapitulation
    M. T. — Main theme
    Codetta

TO THE PIANIST

As you study this movement, write the abbreviations as listed here to identify the various divisions of the form.

Can you analyze each division as to whether the musical idea is REPETITION, CONTRAST or VARIATION?

Moderato grazioso

II

SONG FORM

A — First theme

B — Second theme

A — First theme

C — Extended ending

TO THE PIANIST

As you study this movement, write the capital letters as listed here to identify the various divisions of the form.

Can you analyze each division as to whether the musical idea is REPETITION, CONTRAST or VARIATION?

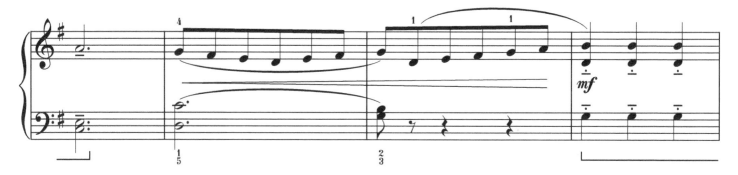

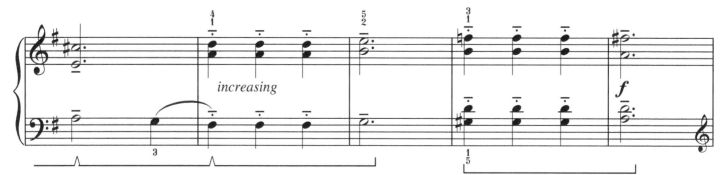

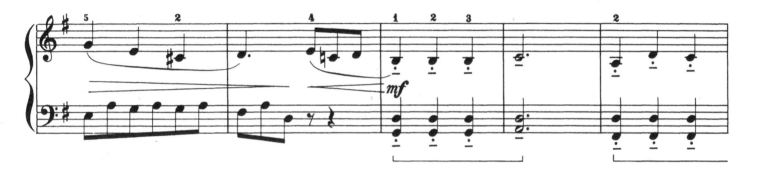

6

III

RONDO FORM

A — First theme

B — Second theme

C — Modulatory sequence

A — Main theme

D — Closing theme

E — Extended theme

TO THE PIANIST

As you study this movement, write the capital letters as listed here to identify the various divisions of the form.

Can you analyze each division as to whether the musical idea is REPETITION, CONTRAST or VARIATION?

Vivace

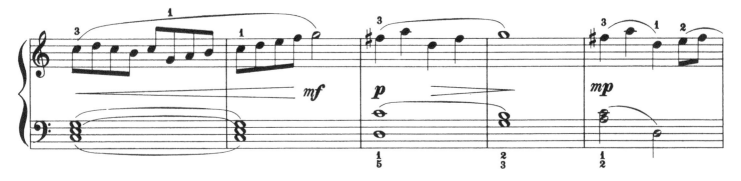

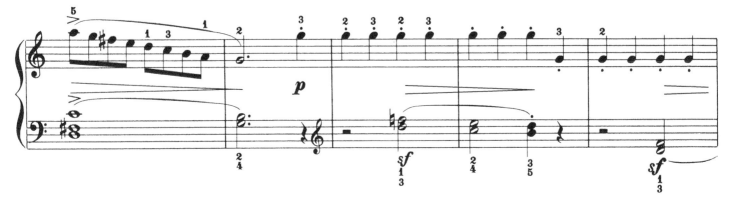

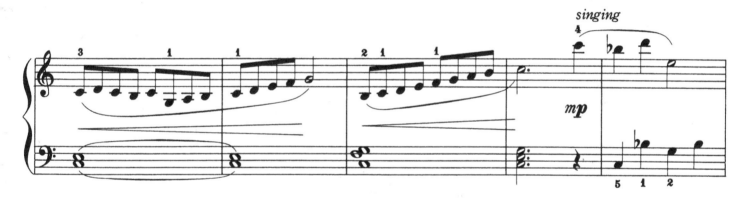

Second Sonatina

I

SONATA FORM

Exposition
   M. T. — Main theme
   S. T. — Sub theme
Development
   D. G. — Development Group
           based on M. T.
   D. G. — Development Group
           based on S. T.
Recapitulation
   M. T. — Main theme
   S. T. — Sub theme
Codetta

TO THE PIANIST

As you study this movement, write the abbreviations as listed here to identify the various divisions of the form.

Can you analyze each division as to whether the musical idea is REPETITION, CONTRAST or VARIATION?

Allegro

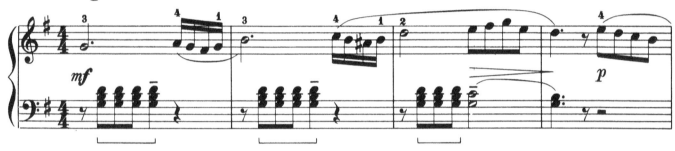

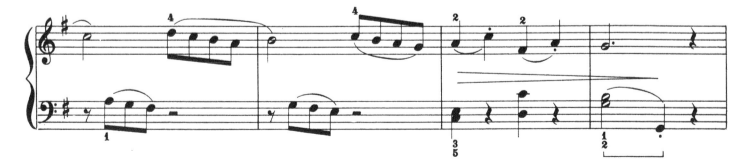

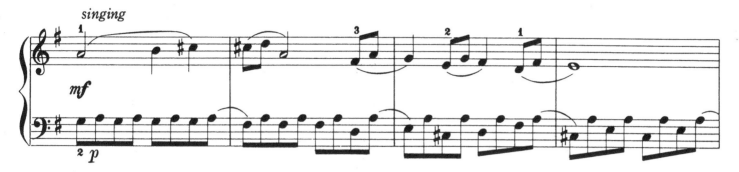

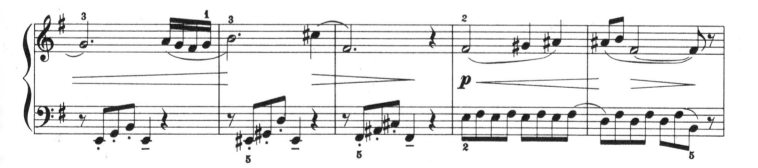

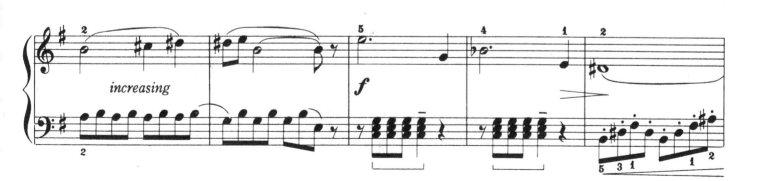

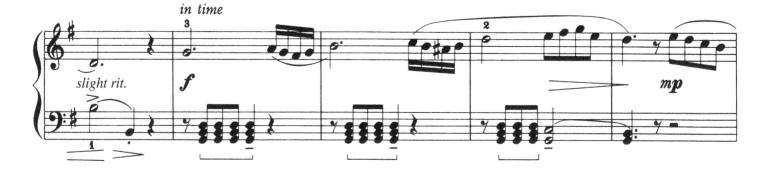

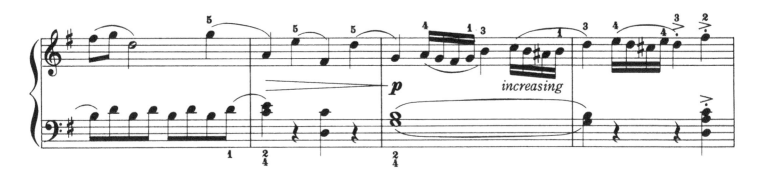

II

SONG FORM

A — First theme (1st statement)

A — First theme (2nd statement)

B — Second theme

A — First theme (2nd statement)

C — Codetta

TO THE PIANIST

As you study this movement, write the abbreviations as listed here to identify the various divisions of the form.

Can you analyze each division as to whether the musical idea is REPETITION, CONTRAST or VARIATION?

Moderato cantabile

III

RONDO FORM

A — First theme
B — Second theme
A — First theme
C — Third theme
D — Modulatory sequence
A — First theme
E — Extended ending

TO THE PIANIST

As you study this movement, write the capital letters as listed here to identify the various divisions of the form.

Can you analyze each division as to whether the musical idea is REPETITION, CONTRAST or VARIATION?

Allegro vivace

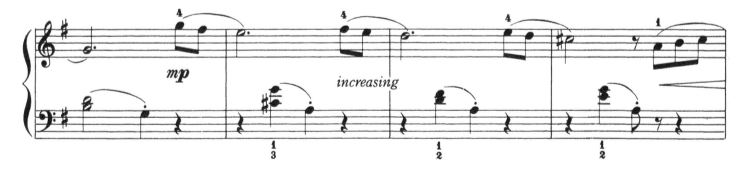

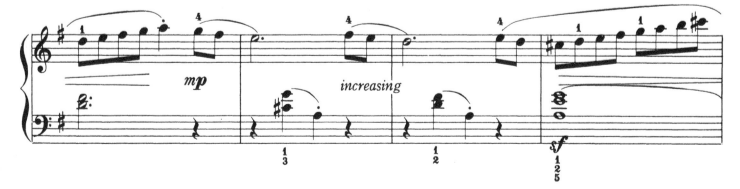

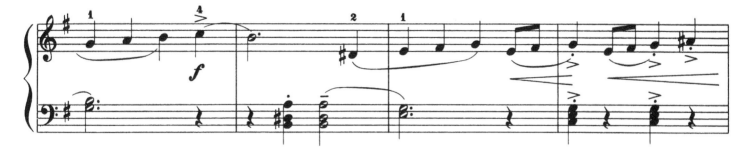

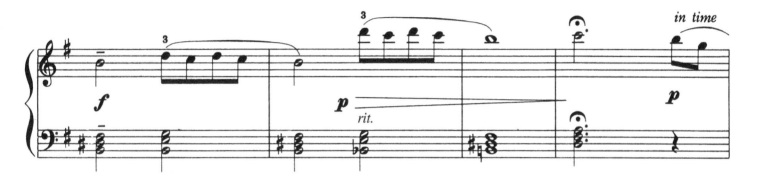

Third Sonatina

I

SONATA FORM

Exposition
    M. T. — Main theme
    S. T. — Sub theme
Modulatory interlude
Development
    D. G. — Development group
           based on M. T.
Recapitulation
    S. T. — Sub theme
Codetta

TO THE PIANIST

As you study this movement, write the capital letters as listed here to identify the various divisions of the form.

Can you analyze each division as to whether the musical idea is REPETITION, CONTRAST or VARIATION?

Allegretto grazioso

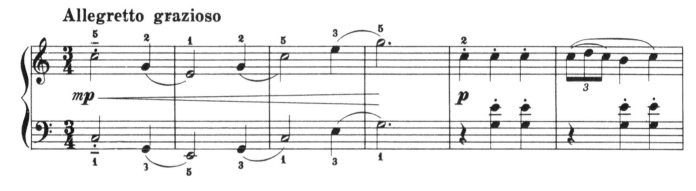

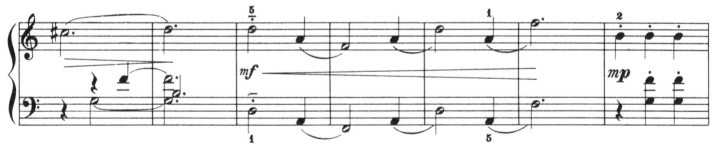

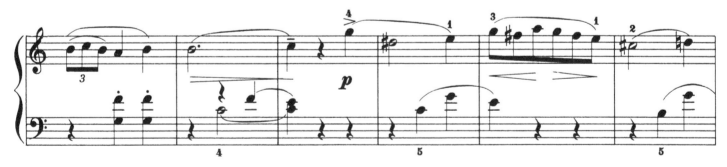

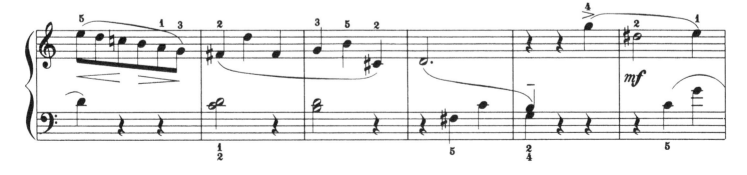

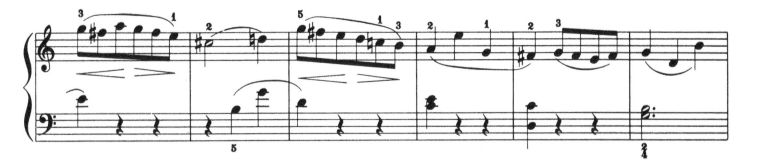

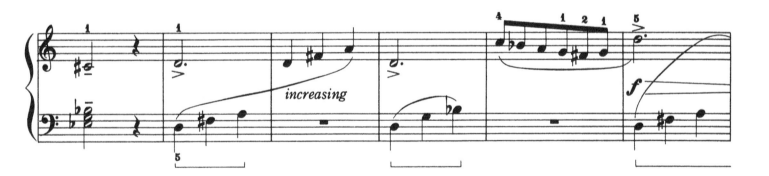

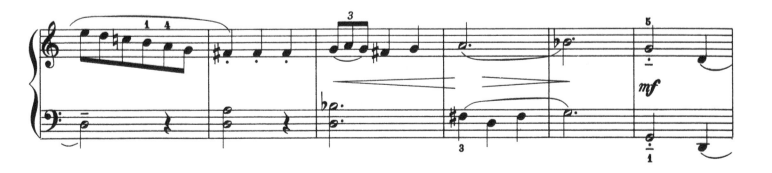

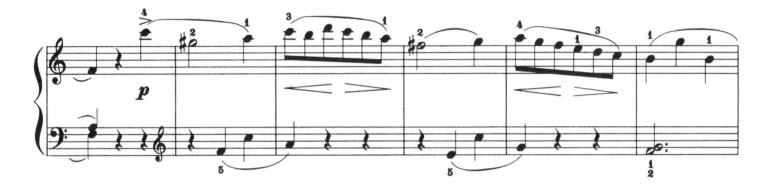

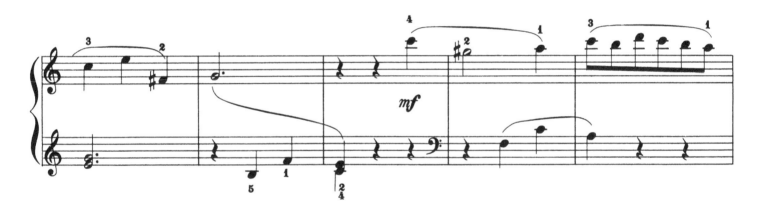

II

DANCE FORM

Minuet
    A — First theme
    B — Second theme

Trio
    A — First theme
    B — Second theme

Coda (identified)

TO THE PIANIST

As you study this movement, write the capital letters as listed here to identify the various divisions of the form.

Can you analyze each division as to whether the musical idea is REPETITION, CONTRAST or VARIATION?

Tempo di menuetto

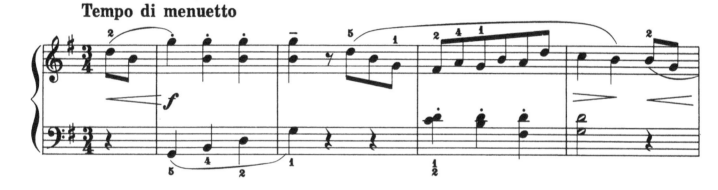

20

Trio

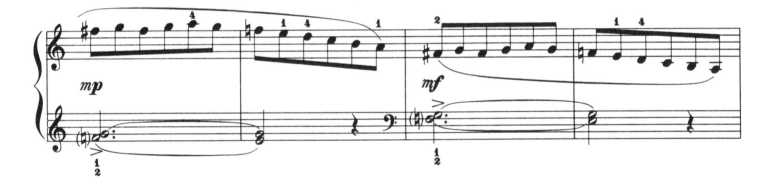

Menuet D. C.

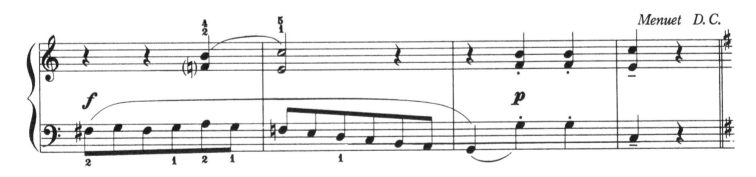

Coda

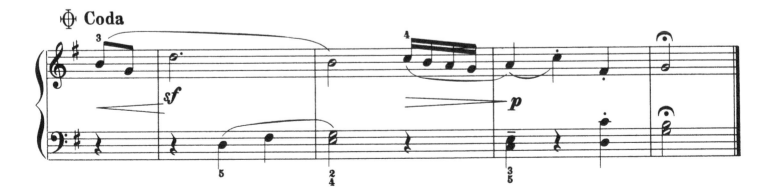

III

RONDO FORM

A — First theme (1st statement)
A — First theme (2nd statement)
B — Second theme
A — First theme (2nd statement)
C — Third theme
A — First theme (1st statement)
A — First theme (2nd statement)
D — Codetta

TO THE PIANIST

As you study this movement, write the capital letters as listed here to identify the various divisions of the form.

Can you analyze each division as to whether the musical idea is REPETITION, CONTRAST or VARIATION?

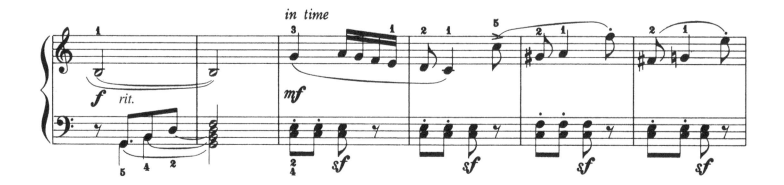

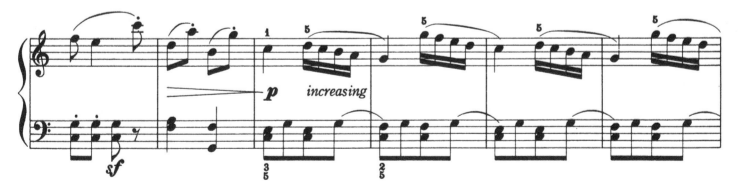

MUSIC FROM
William Gillock

Available exclusively from Willis Music

"The Gillock name spells magic to teachers around the world..."
Lynn Freeman Olson, renowned piano pedagogue

NEW ORLEANS JAZZ STYLES

William Gillock's bestselling *New Orleans Jazz Styles* have been repertoire staples since the 1960s. He believed that every student's musical education should include experiences in a variety of popular styles, including jazz, as a recurring phase of study. Because spontaneity is an essential ingredient of the jazz idiom, performers are encouraged to incorporate their own improvisations.

NEW ORLEANS JAZZ STYLES
Mid-Intermediate
New Orleans Nightfall • The Constant Bass • Mardi Gras • Dixieland Combo • Frankie and Johnny (Theme and Variations).
00415931 Book Only $6.99

MORE NEW ORLEANS JAZZ STYLES
Mid-Intermediate
New Orleans Blues • Taking It Easy • After Midnight • Mister Trumpet Man • Bourbon Street Saturday Night.
00415946 Book Only............... $6.99

STILL MORE NEW ORLEANS JAZZ STYLES
Mid-Intermediate
Mississippi Mud • Uptown Blues • Downtown Beat • Canal Street Blues • Bill Bailey.
00404401 Book Only............... $6.99

NEW ORLEANS JAZZ STYLES – COMPLETE EDITION
Mid to Late Intermediate
This complete collection features updated engravings for all 15 original piano solos. In addition, access to orchestrated online audio files is provided.
00416922 Book/Online Audio...$19.99

NEW ORLEANS JAZZ STYLES DUETS – COMPLETE EDITION
Early to Mid-Intermediate
arr. Glenda Austin
All 15 pieces from Gillock's classic *New Orleans Jazz Styles* series adapted for piano duet! Includes access to audio files online for practice.
00362327 Book/Online Audio ..$14.99

NEW ORLEANS JAZZ STYLES SIMPLIFIED – COMPLETE EDITION
Late Elementary to Early Intermediate
arr. Glenda Austin
All 15 songs from the *New Orleans Jazz Styles* series adapted for easy piano.
00357095 3 Books in One!.......$12.99

ACCENT ON... SERIES

ACCENT ON GILLOCK SERIES
Excellent piano solos for recitals in all levels by Gillock.

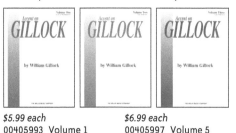

$5.99 each
00405993 Volume 1
00405994 Volume 2
00405995 Volume 3
00405996 Volume 4

$6.99 each
00405997 Volume 5
00405999 Volume 6
00406000 Volume 7
00406001 Volume 8

Complete Edition
00361225 8 Books in One! $24.99

ACCENT ON... REPERTOIRE BOOKS

00415712 **Analytical Sonatinas** Early Intermediate......$7.99
00122148 **Around the World** Early Intermediate........ $8.99
00415797 **Black Keys** Mid-Intermediate.................. $5.99
00416932 **Classical** Early to Mid-Intermediate........... $8.99
00415748 **Majors** Late Elementary........................ $6.99
00415569 **Majors & Minors** Early Intermediate.......... $7.99
00415165 **Rhythm & Style** Mid-Intermediate............. $6.99
00118900 **Seasons** Early Intermediate.................... $8.99
00278505 **Timeless Songs** Early Intermediate.......... $12.99

ACCENT ON DUETS
Mid to Later Intermediate
8 original duets, including: Sidewalk Cafe • Liebesfreud (Kreisler) • Jazz Prelude • Dance of the Sugar Plum Fairy (Tchaikovsky) • Fiesta Mariachi.
00416804 1 Piano/4 Hands $13.99

ACCENT ON SOLOS – COMPLETE
Early to Late Elementary
All 3 of Gillock's popular *Accent on Solos* books. These 33 short teaching pieces continue to motivate piano students of every age!
00200896............................ $14.99

ACCENT ON TWO PIANOS
Intermediate to Advanced
Titles: Carnival in Rio • On a Paris Boulevard • Portrait of Paris • Viennese Rondo. Includes a duplicate score insert for the second piano.
00146176 2 Pianos, 4 Hands..... $12.99

ALSO AVAILABLE

CLASSIC PIANO REPERTOIRE – WILLIAM GILLOCK
Elementary
8 great solos have been re-engraved for this collection: Little Flower Girl of Paris • Spooky Footsteps • On a Paris Boulevard • Stately Sarabande • Rocking Chair Blues • and more!
00416957............................. $8.99

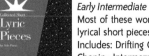

CLASSIC PIANO REPERTOIRE – WILLIAM GILLOCK
Intermediate to Advanced
A dozen delightful pieces have been re-engraved in this collection. Includes favorites such as *Valse Etude, Festive Piece, Polynesian Nocturne,* and *Sonatine.*
00416912............................ $12.99

LYRIC PIECES
Early Intermediate
Most of these wonderfully warm and lyrical short pieces are one-page long. Includes: Drifting Clouds • Homage to Chopin • Intermezzo • Land of Pharaoh • A Memory of Paris • Petite Etude • Summer Clouds • and more.
00405943............................ $7.99

WILLIAM GILLOCK RECITAL COLLECTION
Intermediate to Advanced
Features an extensive compilation of over 50 of William Gillock's most popular and frequently performed recital pieces. Newly engraved and edited to celebrate Gillock's centennial year.
00201747... $19.99

A YOUNG PIANIST'S FIRST BIG NOTE SOLOS
Early to Mid-Intermediate
10 short solos perfect for a student's first recital: Clowns • Glass Slipper • Let's Waltz • The Little Shepherd • New Roller Skates • Pagoda Bells • Smoke Signals • Spooky Footsteps • Swing Your Partner • Water Lilies.
00416229... $6.99

Many more collections, duets and solo sheets available by William Gillock. Search for these and more Willis Music publications for piano at willispianomusic.com.

Find us online at
willispianomusic.com

EXCLUSIVELY DISTRIBUTED BY